**THE STORY OF THE
INDIANAPOLIS COLTS**

THE STORY OF THE INDIANAPOLIS COLTS

NFL TODAY

TYLER OMOTH

CREATIVE EDUCATION

Cover: Colts offense, 1958 (top), quarterback
Peyton Manning (bottom)
Page 2: Quarterback Johnny Unitas
Pages 4–5: 2008 Indianapolis Colts
Pages 6–7: 2006 Indianapolis Colts

....

Published by Creative Education
P.O. Box 227, Mankato, Minnesota 56002
Creative Education is an imprint of
The Creative Company
www.thecreativecompany.us

Design and production by Blue Design
Design Associate: Sarah Yakawonis
Printed in the United States of America

Photographs by AP Images, Corbis (Bettmann,
Bohemian Nomad Picturemakers, Richard
Cummins), Getty Images (Kevin C. Cox, Diamond
Images, Focus On Sport, Chris Graythen, Jeff
Gross, Jeff Haynes/AFP, Tom Hauck, Jed Jacobsohn,
Kidwiler Collection/Diamond Images, Nick Laham,
Streeter Lecka, Andy Lyons, NFL, Darryl Norenberg/
NFL, Doug Pensinger, Al Pereira/NFL, Robert Riger,
Frank Rippon/NFL, Joe Robbins, Eliot Schechter/
Allsport, Marc Serota, Rick Stewart/Allsport, Kevin
Terrell/NFL)

Library of Congress Cataloging-in-Publication Data

Omoth, Tyler.
The story of the Indianapolis Colts / by Tyler
Omoth.
p. cm. — (NFL today)
Includes index.
ISBN 978-1-58341-758-4
1. Indianapolis Colts (Football team)—History—
Juvenile literature. 2. Baltimore Colts (Football
team)—History—Juvenile literature. I. Title. II.
Series.

GV956.I53O66 2008
796.332'640977252—dc22   2008022691

First Edition
9 8 7 6 5 4 3 2 1

CONTENTS

ON THE SIDELINES

MEET THE COLTS

UNITED BY UNITAS

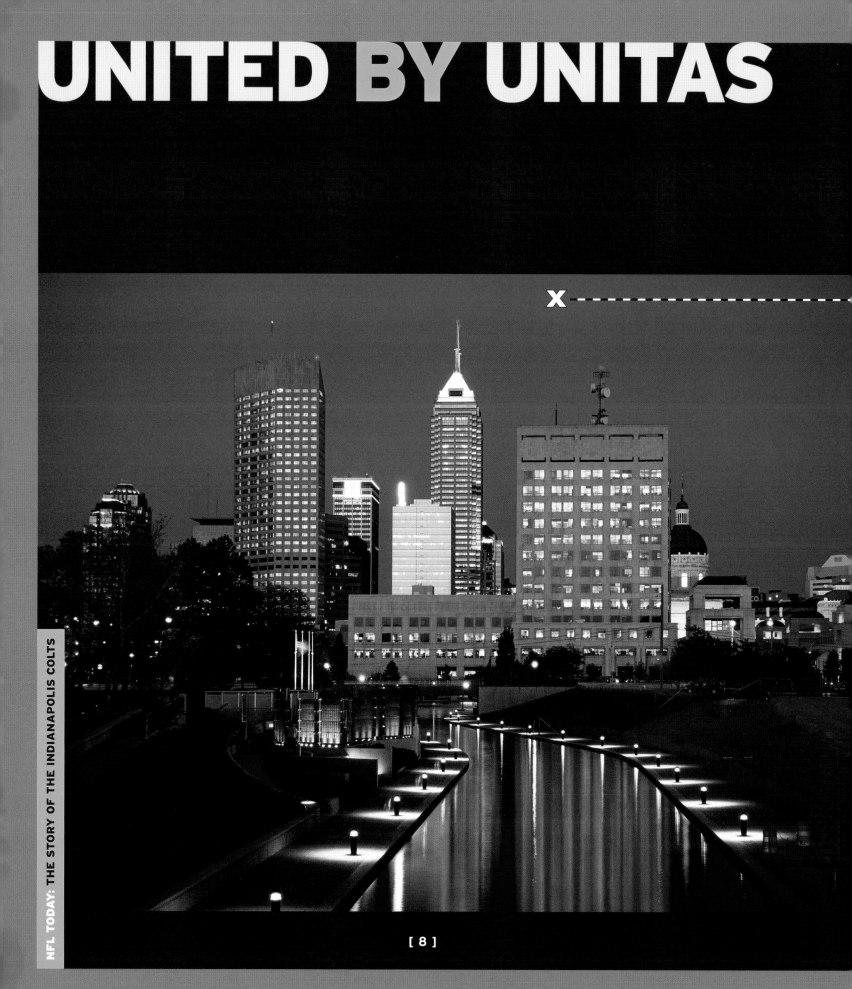

X----------------------------------

The city of Indianapolis, Indiana, started out with just 8,000 people when it was founded in 1850. Today, it features a population of more than 700,000. Sports, especially automobile racing, have played a big part in the history of Indianapolis. The Indianapolis 500, which started in 1911, is the most famous auto race in the world and is still held annually at the Indianapolis Motor Speedway. Many sports fans in Indianapolis and throughout Indiana also pledge their support to the Indiana University Hoosiers athletic teams, as well as to the National Basketball Association's Indiana Pacers franchise.

In 1984, the National Football League (NFL) gave Indiana sports fans yet another reason to cheer. That year, a football team known as the Colts moved west from Baltimore, Maryland, and put down roots in Indianapolis. The Colts brought a long, proud football tradition with them to the Midwest, and they wasted no time in earning a place in the hearts of the Indiana faithful.

The Colts played their first season in Baltimore in 1953 and were led early on by veteran NFL coach Weeb Ewbank. From 1953 to 1955, the Colts went a combined 11–24–1. The team had a few talented players, such as running back Claude "Buddy" Young and defensive back Bert Rechichar, and a

X Although the state of Indiana has long been known as a basketball hotbed, it has also become big-time football country since the Colts arrived in Indianapolis nearly three decades ago.

X Defensive end Gino Marchetti, who would later be enshrined in the Pro Football Hall of Fame, was regarded by many as the finest pure pass rusher in the NFL in the 1950s.

defensive line that was anchored by tackle Art Donovan and defensive end Gino Marchetti. But what the team lacked was an on-field leader. Then, before the 1956 season, an unknown quarterback named Johnny Unitas was brought into training camp for a tryout. The coaching staff was impressed enough with the tough young passer to add him to the roster. Early in the 1956 season, Baltimore's starting quarterback broke his leg. Unitas stepped in and quickly established himself as a star with a knack for producing comeback victories.

Unitas led the Colts to a 7–5 record in 1957. In 1958, Baltimore jumped to 9–3. By then, the team had a high-powered offense that featured Unitas, bruising fullback Alan Ameche, and sure-handed receivers Lenny Moore and Raymond Berry. These players led the charge as the young Colts battled all the way to the 1958 NFL Championship Game, where they faced the New York Giants. Baltimore won the thrilling, back-and-forth contest 23–17 on an overtime touchdown plunge by Ameche, making the Colts NFL champions.

JOHNNY UNITAS

QUARTERBACK
COLTS SEASONS: 1956-72
HEIGHT: 6-FOOT-1
WEIGHT: 194 POUNDS

There may not be a better underdog story in the history of the NFL than that of Johnny Unitas. After the Pittsburgh Steelers selected the young quarterback in the ninth round of the 1955 Draft, the team cut him before the season began. Unitas returned to a life of construction work and playing semi-pro football for a local Pittsburgh team before coach Weeb Ewbank gave him a tryout and signed him to the Colts. After throwing his first NFL pass for an interception, Unitas settled in and became one of the greatest quarterbacks in history. He thrived in high-pressure situations and led the Colts to NFL titles in 1958 and 1959 and a Super Bowl championship in 1970. His black, high-top, boot-style cleats and crew-cut hair became an enduring image of his general-like leadership on the field. Raymond Berry, a favorite target of Unitas's, said that his biggest strengths were "his uncanny instinct of calling the right play at the right time, his icy composure under fire, his fierce competitiveness, and his utter disregard for his own safety."

BIRTH OF THE COLTS

In 1946, a group of investors purchased the Miami Seahawks, a failing team from the All-America Football Conference (AAFC), and brought them to Baltimore. In an effort to help Baltimore embrace its new team, the new ownership asked fans to help rename the franchise. Charles Evans, a Maryland native, won a naming contest with his suggestion to dub the team the "Baltimore Colts," with a horseshoe as its logo. The name was selected as a tribute to Baltimore's proud tradition and history of horse racing. The Preakness Stakes, one of the most prestigious horse races, is held in Baltimore each May. Unfortunately, after the AAFC merged with the NFL in 1950, the Colts posted a miserable 1–11 record, and the league dissolved the team due to its lack of financial stability. Two years went by without professional football in Baltimore. Then, in December 1952, NFL commissioner Bert Bell challenged Baltimore to sell 15,000 season tickets in just 6 weeks. Loyal fans reached that quota in 4 weeks and 3 days, and the Colts were back in business in Baltimore!

In 1959, the Colts again took on the Giants for the championship. The game was close until Unitas sparked the Colts to 24 fourth-quarter points, and Baltimore won in a 31–16 rout. This performance added to the already enormous legend of "Johnny U." "You can't intimidate him," said Los Angeles Rams defensive tackle Merlin Olsen. "He waits until the last possible second to release the ball, even if it means he's going to take a good lick. When he sees us coming, he knows it's going to hurt, and we know it's going to hurt. But he just stands there and takes it. No other quarterback has such class."

The Colts struggled during the early 1960s, posting mediocre records. After the 1962 season, the team decided that a change was necessary and fired Coach Ewbank. In 1963, Baltimore brought in Don Shula, who had played for the Colts as a defensive back during the team's inaugural 1953 season, as its new head coach. Coach Shula's first step in boosting the Colts was to improve the defense. Although the team had several talented defenders, including linebacker Don Shinnick, it needed a spark. With an influx of young talent that included tight end John Mackey and rookie fullback Tony Lorick, Shula guided Unitas and the Colts to a 10-game winning streak in 1964. Baltimore won the Western

X A team captain for most of his 11-season Baltimore career, linebacker Mike Curtis hit hard but also showed soft hands in pass coverage, intercepting a total of 25 passes.

Conference championship with a 12–2 record but lost in the NFL Championship Game to the Cleveland Browns, 27–0.

In 1965, Baltimore drafted hard-hitting linebacker Mike "Mad Dog" Curtis out of Duke University. Curtis made an immediate impact on the Colts—and on opposing players. "We were playing Green Bay," Baltimore linebacker Ted Hendricks later recalled. "[Packers running back] Jim Grabowski was coming through the line, and Mike Curtis gave him a good old-fashioned clothesline shot. Grabowski got up wobbly. One of our guys handed him his helmet. He started heading for our bench. I tapped him on the shoulder and turned him around and said, 'Yours is on the other side, Jim.'" With Curtis knocking opponents silly on defense and the veteran Unitas guiding the offense, Baltimore made it to the playoffs again. This time the Colts lost to the Packers, 13–10, but better times for Baltimore were soon to come.

WEEB EWBANK

COACH
COLTS SEASONS: 1954-62

The Baltimore Colts' second coach, Weeb Ewbank walked the Colts sidelines for nine full seasons. Ewbank was well known for his ability to groom raw, young talent into skilled football players—a talent that made him especially instrumental in the career of quarterback great Johnny Unitas. Ewbank was a master game planner and portrayed a very calm demeanor during the week. That wasn't the case on game days, though. During games, Ewbank would be so jittery that he'd chew ice and spit out the pieces as he watched his game plan unfold in front of him. Ewbank led the Colts to two NFL championships, including the 1958 title game that is commonly called "The Greatest Game Ever Played." After leaving the Colts in 1963, Ewbank went on to coach the New York Jets to a shocking victory over the Colts in Super Bowl III, becoming the only coach to win both NFL and American Football League (AFL) championship titles as well as a Super Bowl. "I played under 9 head coaches and 42 assistants," recalled Jets Hall of Fame wide receiver Don Maynard, "and nobody ever did it as good as Weeb."

A PAIR OF SUPER BOWLS

The Colts went 13–1 and won the NFL championship in 1968. Earlier in the decade, that would have been the ultimate accomplishment. But 1968 was the third year that the NFL champion had faced the champion of the rival AFL in a Super Bowl to determine an undisputed world champion. The Colts were heavily favored to beat the New York Jets in Super Bowl III. But in one of the most famous upsets in sports history, the Jets and their star quarterback, Joe Namath, handed the Colts a 16–7 defeat.

The Colts bounced back from the loss with determination and returned to the Super Bowl two years later, this time to face the Dallas Cowboys. The Colts trailed 13–6 at halftime and found themselves without Unitas, who had suffered a rib injury. But backup quarterback Earl Morrall led the offense down the field for a tying touchdown late in the fourth quarter, and Curtis then intercepted a Dallas pass. Three plays later, rookie kicker Jim O'Brien booted a field goal to give the Colts a 16–13 win and their fourth NFL championship. "I don't remember any noise," O'Brien said of his big moment, "I don't remember seeing Earl Morrall, who was the holder. There was no sound. I didn't even see the ground, all I saw was the ball."

The Colts made the playoffs in 1971 but were beaten by the Miami Dolphins. That was the last hurrah for many of the

X Two years after his team suffered an upset loss in Super Bowl III, Johnny Unitas helped the Colts win Super Bowl V by tossing a touchdown pass before being knocked out of the game.

great Colts players of the '60s. When the Colts finished the 1972 season 5–9, it was clear that the team needed some new blood. After the season, new team owner Robert Irsay decided to trade Unitas to the San Diego Chargers. Unitas left Baltimore as the NFL's all-time leader in pass completions (2,796), passing yards (39,768), and touchdown passes (287).

In 1973, the Colts found their new quarterback in the NFL Draft, selecting Louisiana State University star Bert Jones. The young quarterback spent his first two seasons on the bench, but by 1975, he was ready to step into the starting role. Jones proved to be a worthy replacement for Unitas by leading the Colts to a 10–4 record and their first American Football Conference (AFC) East Division title.

Jones quickly earned the respect of his teammates with his leadership and toughness. In one 1976 game, Jones led the Colts to a victory over the Houston Oilers despite having a terrible case of the flu. "He was so sick yesterday that I thought he'd fall down if an Oiler so much as breathed on him," said Baltimore offensive lineman George Kuntz after the game. "But he played another great game. He's tough. It kind of rubs off on the rest of us."

The 1976 season got off to a rocky start, as a dispute between team owner Robert Irsay and head coach Ted

X One of the toughest quarterbacks of all time (and boasting one of the strongest throwing arms ever), Bert Jones earned NFL Most Valuable Player (MVP) honors in 1976.

THE GREATEST GAME EVER PLAYED

Most football games last until the clock runs out. But the 1958 NFL Championship Game between the Baltimore Colts and the New York Giants would remain in the memories of football fans for decades. Still known to this day as "The Greatest Game Ever Played," this famous showdown took place on December 28 at Yankee Stadium in New York City. With only two minutes left in the game and the Giants leading 17–14, the Colts had the ball on their own 14-yard line. Colts quarterback Johnny Unitas, who excelled in high-pressure situations, engineered a drive that allowed kicker Steve Myhra to boot the tying field goal with just seven seconds left. America was about to witness the very first NFL Championship Game to be decided by sudden-death overtime. After holding the Giants in overtime, the Colts drove 80 yards to score on a 1-yard run by running back Alan Ameche. Watched by millions of fans on television, The Greatest Game Ever Played was credited with sparking broad interest in professional football and helping it become arguably the most popular spectator sport in America.

Marchibroda (Shula had left Baltimore in 1970) led to the popular coach's resignation. After Colts players voiced their disapproval and threatened to walk out, Marchibroda was reinstated. Behind Jones, the Colts went on to win the AFC East with an 11–3 record but were shut down in the playoffs by the Pittsburgh Steelers, 40–14.

Baltimore once again won the AFC East in 1977, but it took a 30–24 victory over the New England Patriots in the final game of the season to claim the divisional crown. Once again, though, the Colts were knocked out of the playoffs in the first round, this time 37–31 in a double-overtime loss to the Oakland Raiders. Although the postseason losses were frustrating, Baltimore fans continued to believe that their team would soon break through to championship glory. Unfortunately, things would get worse for the Colts before they would get better.

From 1978 to 1983, the Colts struggled, posting losing records every year. In 1983, the team was forced to trade away its top draft pick (and the first choice overall), quarterback John Elway, because he refused to play for a team that he believed showed no promise. After the 1983 season, investors from Indianapolis approached Irsay about moving his team to their city. Irsay looked at Indianapolis's Hoosier Dome,

GINO MARCHETTI

DEFENSIVE END
COLTS SEASONS: 1953-64
HEIGHT: 6-FOOT-4
WEIGHT: 244 POUNDS

The last thing a quarterback in the 1950s wanted was a third-and-long situation with Gino Marchetti staring at him from across the line of scrimmage. For more than a decade, Marchetti was one of the NFL's most feared pass rushers, and before that, he was a machine gunner during the famous Battle of the Bulge in World War II. Known as a violent hitter yet a clean player, Marchetti was a great all-around defensive end, but he was at his best in passing situations. In 1954, Marchetti protected Colts quarterbacks as a converted offensive tackle, but soon he was moved back to the other side of the line. Many teams chose to double- or even triple-team him with blockers to protect their passer, but that only opened up opportunities for Marchetti's defensive teammates. He suffered his first serious injury, a broken leg, during the Colts' dramatic 1958 NFL Championship Game victory, forcing him to miss the Pro Bowl. That was the only gap in what would have been 11 straight Pro Bowl appearances for the legendary pass rusher.

a brand-new, 60,000-seat domed stadium, and after his attempts to get a new stadium in Baltimore were rebuffed, he decided to make the move. One night, moving vans showed up at the team's Baltimore headquarters, and the Colts bolted for Indiana.

The move broke the hearts of many faithful Baltimore fans, but sports fans in Indiana enthusiastically welcomed the team, even as it continued to struggle in the mid-1980s. Then, in 1987, the Colts traded for star running back Eric Dickerson. Known for his graceful yet hard-nosed running style, Dickerson had established himself as one of the league's top rushers with the Los Angeles Rams.

Dickerson joined a Colts offense that already featured deep-threat wide receiver Bill Brooks and outstanding linemen Ray Donaldson and Chris Hinton. This collection of players helped carry the 1987 Colts to a 9–6 record, an AFC East title, and their first playoff appearance in 10 years. "This year, it all came true," said Donaldson. "All the dreams we had before." Unfortunately, the Colts' playoff run was short-lived, as the Cleveland Browns defeated Indianapolis 38–21.

FROM MARCHIBRODA TO MANNING

In 1988, Dickerson charged for a franchise-record 1,659 yards as the Colts went 9–7 and just missed the playoffs. But after that, Indianapolis began to stumble. Over the next two seasons, the Colts went 8–8 and 7–9. In 1991, the team collapsed completely with an embarrassing 1–15 record. It was time to rebuild the Colts.

In 1992, Ted Marchibroda, who had coached the Colts in Baltimore, was hired to re-energize the franchise. Marchibroda believed that coaching was "a 24-hour-a-day job. No motivating speech is going to make a difference. You have to work with your football team every minute to get it ready to play on Sunday."

Marchibroda's commitment paid off as the Colts jumped to 9–7 in 1992. The team slumped to 4–12 a year later, but Indianapolis then made two key off-season moves that would give the team a major boost. First, it signed veteran quarterback Jim Harbaugh. Then, it drafted Marshall Faulk—

One of the all-time greats, Eric Dickerson made NFL history in 1989 by becoming the first running back ever to rush for more than 1,000 yards in 7 straight seasons. **X**

an all-purpose running back known for his quick acceleration and shifty moves—in the first round of the 1994 NFL Draft.

In 1995, these players propelled the Colts back to the playoffs for a magical run. First, they upset the defending AFC champion San Diego Chargers 35–20. Then they beat the powerful Kansas City Chiefs 10–7. The excitement finally came to an end in the AFC Championship Game, when the Colts lost a 20–16 heartbreaker to the Steelers. On the last play of the game, Harbaugh launched a "Hail Mary" pass that was nearly caught by Colts receiver Aaron Bailey for a touchdown.

The Colts again put together a 9–7 record and made the playoffs in 1996. A matchup against Pittsburgh in round one gave the Colts a chance to avenge the previous year's defeat, but the Steelers overwhelmed the Colts, 42–14.

When the Colts slipped to 3–13 in 1997, the team was put in the hands of former New Orleans Saints head coach Jim Mora. With Mora at the helm, the Colts used the first overall pick in the 1998 NFL Draft to add a new quarterback: University of Tennessee star Peyton Manning, the son of former NFL quarterback Archie Manning.

In 1998, the Colts again went just 3–13. Manning showed signs of stardom, though, and began to build a great on-field relationship with speedy receiver Marvin Harrison that would last for many years. "He's the kind of guy who wants to be

THE BLUNDER BOWL

When the box score shows that a football team threw three interceptions, lost four fumbles, and had its leading rusher gain only 33 yards, it's a bad sign. That's not exactly a recipe for a win—unless the team is the 1970 Baltimore Colts, and the game is Super Bowl V. Filled with sloppy play, turnovers, and even some officiating mistakes, Super Bowl V is sometimes called "The Blunder Bowl." In the first quarter, Colts quarterback Johnny Unitas threw a pass that ricocheted off Baltimore receiver Eddie Hinton's fingertips, was tipped by Dallas Cowboys defensive back Mel Renfro, and then was snatched out of the air by Baltimore tight end John Mackey for a 75-yard touchdown reception. In the third quarter, Hinton grabbed a pass that was intended for Mackey, only to fumble the ball at the 10-yard line and see it get batted through the end zone for a touchback. The Cowboys gave the ball back promptly with an interception just three plays later. Eventually, improved play by the Colts defense and a clutch kick by Jim O'Brien gave Baltimore the victory.

coached," Coach Mora said of Manning. "You can't overwork him. He's like a sponge. He wants to do the best he can, and he wants you to give him all that you have to give him."

With budding superstars at quarterback and wide receiver, the Colts continued to add talent. In 1999, they traded Faulk to the St. Louis Rams and then selected explosive University of Miami running back Edgerrin James in the NFL Draft. Indianapolis also built up its defense by signing veteran linebacker Cornelius Bennett and end Chad Bratzke.

The off-season moves paid off as the Colts skyrocketed to a 13–3 record in 1999. Manning, Harrison, and James became perhaps the most feared offensive trio in the NFL: Manning threw for more than 4,000 yards, Harrison led all NFL receivers with 1,663 yards, and James led the league in rushing with 1,553 yards. The season came to a disappointing end in the playoffs, though, as the Colts lost 19–16 to the Tennessee Titans.

When the Colts slumped to 6–10 in 2001, Coach Mora was replaced by Tony Dungy, a defense-minded coach who had previously built the Tampa Bay Buccaneers into a powerhouse. The Colts surged to 10–6 in their first season under Dungy, thanks in part to young defensive end Dwight Freeney, receiver Reggie Wayne, and tight end Marcus Pollard. Unfortunately, the season again ended on a bitter note as they were drubbed 41–0 by the Jets in the playoffs.

BACK TO THE BIG GAME

In 2003, the Colts bolstered their already fearsome passing game by drafting tight end Dallas Clark out of the University of Iowa. They also got a big boost from kicker Mike Vanderjagt, who set a league record by going an entire season and postseason without missing a field goal or an extra-point attempt. Thanks in part to Clark and Vanderjagt, the Colts assembled a 12–4 record. Unfortunately, Indianapolis came up short once again in its bid to reach the Super Bowl, losing to the New England Patriots in the AFC Championship Game—a loss that began an intense rivalry between the clubs that would last for years.

In 2004, Manning put together one of the greatest seasons any quarterback has ever achieved. He was given the NFL's Most Valuable Player (MVP) award after throwing a league-record 49 touchdown passes and racking up 4,557 passing yards. "It's difficult to pick one player out of the league and determine who is the most valuable," said Coach Dungy. "But Peyton sets the tempo for us. We ask a lot of him, and he's certainly delivered."

JOHN MACKEY

TIGHT END
COLTS SEASONS: 1963-71
HEIGHT: 6-FOOT-2
WEIGHT: 224 POUNDS

In the early 1960s, tight ends were used mainly as extra blockers on the offensive line. John Mackey added a whole new element to the position with his spectacular ball-catching skills and field-stretching speed. In fact, Mackey was so fast that the Colts even used him as a kickoff return specialist. His athleticism and speed created headaches for opposing defenses and helped Mackey make it to the Pro Bowl five times during his career. During Super Bowl V, after the 1970 season, Mackey was part of one of the most memorable plays in Super Bowl history. Colts quarterback Johnny Unitas tried to complete a pass to wide receiver Eddie Hinton, only to have Hinton deflect the ball. The ball then brushed the fingers of a Dallas Cowboys defensive back and ended up in Mackey's waiting arms. Mackey took his lucky find 75 yards for a touchdown, putting the Colts in position to eventually win the game on a last-second field goal. Such plays helped Mackey elevate the profile of the tight end position and earned him induction into the Pro Football Hall of Fame in 1992.

Behind Manning's record-setting performance, the Colts again went 12–4 in 2004. Along the way, the wide receiver trio of Harrison, Wayne, and Brandon Stokley became the first NFL threesome to each post more than 1,000 yards and make 10 or more touchdown catches for one team in one season. On the other side of the ball, Freeney used his frightening speed and spin moves to become the first Colts player since 1982 to win the league's sack title, with 16. "Freeney gets better and better every year, and it seems like he's getting faster and faster," Titans quarterback Steve McNair said. "Sometimes you think there's something wrong with the [film] projector when you see how quick he is."

X Star passer Peyton Manning had the luxury of handing off to such great backs as Edgerrin James and Joseph Addai (pictured).

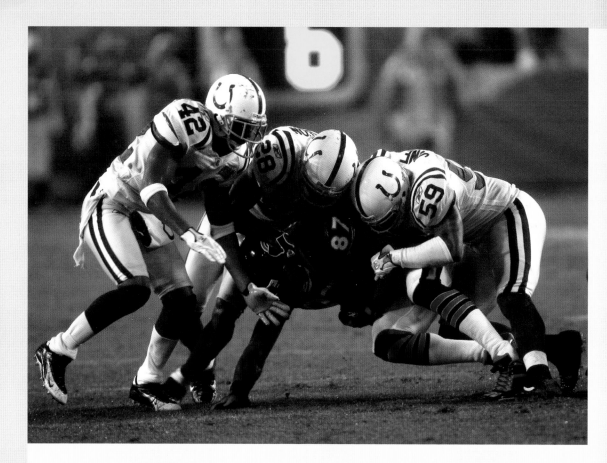

X The Colts were best known for their high-octane offense, but their defense could also flex its muscle; in 2005, Indianapolis surrendered the second-lowest point total in the league.

Despite all of these remarkable individual accomplishments, the Colts were not ready for the Super Bowl just yet. After beating the Denver Broncos 49–24 in their first playoff game, they were stifled by the Patriots a week later, losing 20–3.

The Colts roared to a 14–2 record the next season, due partly to an improved defense that featured aggressive linebacker Cato June and hard-hitting free safety Bob Sanders. Yet despite having home-field advantage throughout the AFC playoffs, the "Horseshoes" again came up short in the postseason, suffering a wrenching, 21–18 loss to the Steelers.

Before the start of the 2006 season, the Colts parted ways with Edgerrin James and let the one-two punch of Dominic Rhodes and rookie Joseph Addai carry the rushing

THE MIDNIGHT MOVE

The early 1980s were a low point for the Baltimore Colts. After several seasons of few victories and low fan attendance, the once-proud franchise's best hope was to build a new stadium to attract new fans and generate increased revenue. But the Colts' owner, Robert Irsay, struggled to convince the city of Baltimore to help the team build a new stadium, and he threatened to move the team. On March 28, 1984, the state of Maryland passed an imminent domain law that would have allowed the city of Baltimore to claim ownership of the team. Afraid that his franchise and his investment were in danger, Irsay quickly agreed to move the Colts to Indianapolis. Under the cover of night, all team property was loaded into Mayflower Transit Company moving trucks. On the morning of March 30, 1984, Baltimore fans were stunned to discover that they no longer had a team. The Colts began a new era in Indianapolis, and Baltimore was left longing for an NFL franchise until 1996, when the Cleveland Browns moved there and became the Baltimore Ravens.

PEYTON MANNING

QUARTERBACK
COLTS SEASONS: 1998-PRESENT
HEIGHT: 6-FOOT-5
WEIGHT: 230 POUNDS

As the son of former NFL quarterback Archie Manning, Peyton Manning came into the league with high expectations placed upon him. Yet after the Colts selected him with the top overall pick in the 1998 Draft, he quickly met—then exceeded—those expectations. The tall, young quarterback set league rookie records for passing yards (3,739) and pass completions (326). An intelligent leader, Manning helped turn the formerly struggling Colts into a perennial contender. In February 2007, he earned the Super Bowl MVP trophy after leading the Colts to victory over the Bears in Super Bowl XLI. As charismatic off the field as he was talented on it, Manning could be seen as a product pitchman in numerous (and often comical) television commercials. And although his abilities on the field were undeniable, it was his dedication and leadership that won over his teammates, coaches, and fans. "You know, a lot of guys talk about wanting to be great," said Colts offensive coordinator Tom Moore. "But Peyton, he does what you have to do with his work ethic, his preparation, and just hard work." After the 2008 season, Manning was named NFL MVP for the third time in his career.

[36]

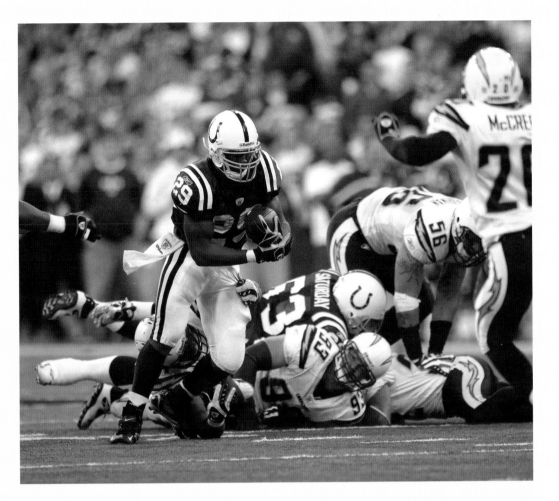

load. Indianapolis also let Vanderjagt leave as a free agent and signed clutch kicker Adam Vinatieri away from the rival Patriots. The result was a 12–4 record and another playoff berth. In the postseason, the Colts toppled the Kansas City Chiefs by a score of 23–8, then took down the Baltimore Ravens 15–6 as Vinatieri booted five field goals. Once again, the Colts would have to defeat the Patriots if they were to reach the Super Bowl.

Behind a strong running attack from Addai and Rhodes and an 80-yard scoring drive in the fourth quarter engineered

X Rookie Joseph Addai came up big in his first postseason game, rushing for 122 yards to help Indianapolis's surge toward Super Bowl XLI.

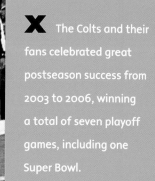

by Manning, the Colts finally toppled the Patriots, winning the AFC Championship Game 38–34 and securing a place in Super Bowl XLI. The showdown, played in Miami, was to be a historic one, as it was the first Super Bowl to feature two teams led by African American head coaches. Tony Dungy brought his Colts to face Lovie Smith and his Chicago Bears.

Bears receiver Devin Hester returned the game's opening kickoff 92 yards across a rain-sodden field for a quick touchdown and an early lead for Chicago. After a first half

X Star kicker Adam Vinatieri booted three field goals to help the Colts topple his old team, the Patriots, in the 2006 AFC Championship Game.

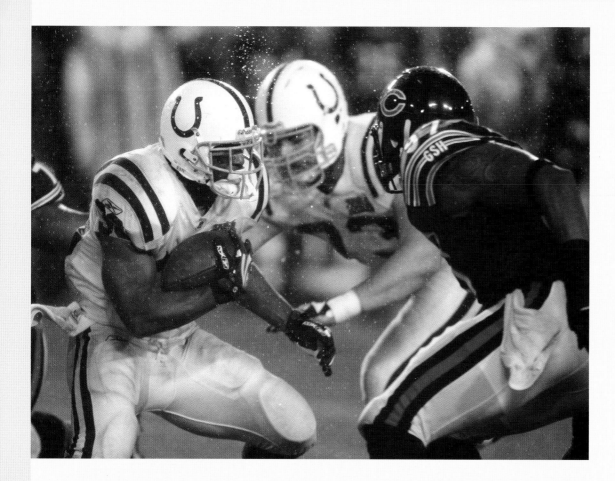

X In one of the rainiest Super Bowls ever, the Colts wore down the physical Bears defense with their own physical rushing attack to capture the world championship.

that was sloppily played by both teams and featured six total turnovers, the Colts held a 16–14 lead. In the second half, thanks to Manning's consistent play, a dominant running game, and an opportunistic defense, the Colts shook off the rain and the Bears to win 29–17 and finally bring the Lombardi Trophy to Indianapolis. Coach Dungy praised his team after the victory, saying, "This may not be our best team in five years, but it was the closest and the most connected—and it showed in the way we played."

The Colts kept their momentum going the next two seasons. In 2007, they went 13–3 to earn a first-round bye in

A QUARTERBACK DEBATE

One was brash, bold, and full of promise. The other was polite, humble, and also full of promise. As the 1998 NFL Draft approached, it was the talk of the sports world. The Colts had the number-one overall pick, but would they choose the pedal-to-the-metal attitude of Washington State University quarterback Ryan Leaf, or University of Tennessee quarterback Peyton Manning, the polished son of former NFL quarterback Archie Manning? By most accounts, Manning was the safe choice, while Leaf's raw talent and confident attitude made him the high-risk, high-reward pick. Indianapolis chose Manning and was glad for it. Leaf, who was chosen second overall by the San Diego Chargers, played erratically and was constantly embroiled in controversies off the field; he threw his last NFL pass in 2001. "Everything you had heard was that Leaf was the far better athlete," recalled Colts president Bill Polian. "Just the opposite was true when you watched the workout. It drove home the idea that you better go through the process." What had looked like a close call wasn't so close after all.

ON THE SIDELINES

ORCHESTRATED CONFUSION

In the early seasons of the 21st century, when the Colts would break the huddle (if they even huddled at all), they would frequently still have about 20 seconds left on the play clock. Then, as the players got into their stances, star quarterback Peyton Manning would run back and forth at the line of scrimmage, yelling and gesticulating wildly to his teammates in what looked like mass confusion. In reality, the Colts' offense, developed by coordinator Tom Moore, was not as complicated as it looked. Manning would call two to four play options in the huddle, and then, once he'd seen the defensive alignment at the line of scrimmage, he would choose and communicate which of those plays he wanted to run. The Colts' offense became so adept at this that players could even communicate the plays with simple hand gestures. Meanwhile, Manning would go through a wide variety of calls and gestures to try to confuse the defense. "My base philosophy has been that players make plays," said Moore. "As a coach, you give them a system that allows them to do that."

the playoffs. There would be no Super Bowl repeat, though. Injuries to such stars as Freeney and Harrison hampered the team, and Indianapolis fell to the Chargers, 28–24. The Colts started slowly in 2008—losing their first two home games in Indianapolis's brand-new Lucas Oil Stadium—but came on strong late in the season to finish 12–4 and earn a Wild Card spot in the playoffs. Unfortunately for Indianapolis fans, the Colts still could not find a way past the Chargers in the postseason, losing 23–17. That game turned out to be the last for Coach Dungy, who then retired and turned the team over to assistant coach Jim Caldwell.

X As several Colts stars went down with injuries in 2007, young players such as linebacker Freddie Keiaho (number 54) picked up the slack.

X Lightning-quick end Dwight Freeney signed a $72-million contract in 2007, then the richest ever for a defensive player.

MARVIN HARRISON

WIDE RECEIVER
COLTS SEASONS: 1996-2008
HEIGHT: 6 FEET
WEIGHT: 185 POUNDS

In the NFL today, it's common to see wide receivers competing over who can come up with the most outlandish touchdown celebrations and crowd-pleasing dances. Yet while many receivers spent time practicing their dance moves, Marvin Harrison quietly kept breaking records. There was very little that was flashy about Harrison. He played smart, ran precise routes, and caught passes—a lot of them. Over the course of his career, he and quarterback Peyton Manning teamed up to become one of the most successful "pitch-and-catch" tandems in NFL history. The pair knew each other so well that, with just a look, they could switch plays to exploit a flaw in the defense. Although Harrison became the Colts' record holder in nearly every receiving category, the quiet star preferred to let his play speak for him, letting more outgoing teammates get most of the media attention. Donovan McNabb, a teammate of Harrison's at Syracuse University and the quarterback for the Philadelphia Eagles, appreciated his style, saying, "So many receivers go throughout their career talking about how great they are, and how much they're going to do. Marvin just does it."

The history of the Colts is a rich one that spans six decades and includes two great sports cities. Over the years, fans in Baltimore have cheered on such legends as Raymond Berry and Johnny Unitas, and fans in Indianapolis have supported such football heroes as Eric Dickerson and Peyton Manning. Now, with a fifth NFL championship recently added to their trophy case, the Indianapolis Colts are aiming to become a new NFL dynasty.

X Although he stood only 5-foot-8, safety Bob Sanders was a 205-pound dynamo who always seemed to play much bigger than his size.

INDEX